Lincoln Township Public Library

s Rd.

127

D1233339

MODERN ROLE MODELS

Tobey Maguire

Terri Dougherty

Lincoln Township Public Library
2099 W. John Beers Rd.
Stevensville, MI 49127
(269) 429-9575

Mason Crest Publishers

Produced by OTTN Publishing in association with
21st Century Publishing and Communications, Inc.

Copyright © 2009 by Mason Crest Publishers. All rights reserved. No part of this
publication may be reproduced or transmitted in any form or by any means,
electronic or mechanical, including photocopying, recording, taping, or any
information storage and retrieval system, without permission from the publisher.

MASON CREST PUBLISHERS INC.
370 Reed Road
Broomall, Pennsylvania 19008
(866) MCP-BOOK (toll free)
www.masoncrest.com

Printed in the United States of America.

First Printing

9 8 7 6 5 4 3 2 1

Library of Congress Cataloging-in-Publication Data

Dougherty, Terri.
   Tobey Maguire / by Terri Dougherty.
      p. cm. — (Modern role models)
   ISBN 978-1-4222-0505-1 — ISBN 978-1-4222-0792-5 (pbk.)
   1. Maguire, Tobey, 1975–   2. Motion picture actors and actresses—United
States—Biography—Juvenile literature. I. Title.
PN2287.M24D68 2008
791.4302'8092—dc22
[B]   2008021354

Publisher's note:
All quotations in this book come from original sources, and contain the spelling
and grammatical inconsistencies of the original text.

CROSS-CURRENTS

*In the ebb and flow of the currents of life we are each influenced
by many people, places, and events that we directly experience
or have learned about. Throughout the chapters of this book you
will come across **CROSS-CURRENTS** reference boxes. These
boxes direct you to a **CROSS-CURRENTS** section in the back
of the book that contains fascinating and informative sidebars
and related pictures. Go on.* ▸▸

CONTENTS

Apple bks 090106

THE BATTLE WITHIN.

A promotional poster for the 2007 film *Spider-Man 3*. During its time in theaters, the movie earned almost $900 million worldwide. This made *Spider-Man 3* the most successful of the Spider-Man films so far. Tobey Maguire has drawn praise for his portrayal of the tough but sensitive comic-book superhero in all three films.

1

He Is Spider-Man

WITH A FLICK OF HIS WRIST, SPIDER-MAN SPINS webs that send him flying between buildings. He soars toward a beautiful girl who needs his help. Dodging chunks of falling concrete, he grabs her in midair. Dangling from a web, he sets her safely on the ground. There is no shortage of excitement when Spider-Man is on the screen.

Spinning a web of thrills and leaping from building to building, Tobey Maguire has leaped to stardom as Spider-Man. When he took on the **role** for the third time, fans expected action, emotion, and great **villains**. Maguire delivered in *Spider-Man 3*. The movie had plenty of excitement and bad guys who were as interesting as they were evil. To top it all off, Spidey had to battle the good and bad he felt within himself.

Fans flock to the theater when Maguire plays Spider-Man. When *Spider-Man 3* was released in May 2007, the film broke box-office records. It brought in more money in a single day than any other movie ever had. In its first weekend it brought in more than $151 million in North America and more than $380 million worldwide. The movie's popularity caused one magazine to comment:

> **It seems fans everywhere can identify with their superhero's latest challenge: battling the evil within himself.**

➤ SPIDEY'S SAGA BEGINS ◄

Maguire's popularity as Spider-Man began with the first movie in the series. He began playing the comic-book hero in the **blockbuster** film *Spider-Man* in 2002. The movie brought in $114 million in its first weekend and established Maguire as a superstar.

The first *Spider-Man* movie introduced audiences to Peter Parker, a teen who gains superpowers after he is bitten by a radioactive spider. As Spider-Man, he can leap great distances and spin webs. He also finds that he has super strength.

Maguire was drawn to the role because of Spider-Man's thoughtful nature. Spider-Man has to deal with the death of his uncle, and he finds out that his best friend's father is evil. In addition, he struggles with his love for his friend Mary Jane.

Action is also a hallmark of the *Spider-Man* movies. In *Spider-Man*, the hero battles the Green Goblin. He fights to save both Mary Jane and a tram car packed with children.

CROSS-CURRENTS
To find out more about the villains Tobey had to face in his superhero role, read "Spider-Man's Enemies." Go to page 46.

Audiences soon learn that it is more than superpowers that make Spider-Man special. He saves the day but realizes that becoming a superhero has not made his life any easier. He learns that with great power comes great responsibility.

➤ SPIDEY'S DECISION ◄

Maguire again took on the role of Spider-Man in 2004. In *Spider-Man 2*, the hero is struggling. Busy with superhero duties, he cannot hold on to a pizza delivery job, has trouble paying his rent, and cannot get close to the girl he loves. Maguire describes the character as being

> **pretty stressed out. He's growing weary of his lifestyle. He's dying to live a normal life.**

Tobey Maguire—wearing his Spider-Man costume—speaks with Mary Jane Watson (played by Kirsten Dunst) in a scene from the original *Spider-Man* film. In the films, Tobey's character often struggles to find the right way to express his feelings for Mary Jane. The doubts and difficulties experienced by Peter Parker make the character seem more realistic.

Peter Parker learns that he cannot look the other way when people are in trouble. In a suspense-filled battle, Spider-Man faces Dr. Otto Octavius. The evil scientist has mechanical arms with a mind of their own.

The original *Spider-Man* was a tough act to follow, but the **sequel** was even better. It took in $200 million at the box office in only eight days. Maguire's portrayal earned him a Saturn Award for Best Actor and a Kids' Choice Award.

⇒ NEW CHALLENGES FOR SPIDER-MAN ⇐

Plans were being made for the third *Spider-Man* movie while the second one was still in theaters. The third movie had a huge **budget**

CROSS-CURRENTS

For more information about Tobey Maguire's director in the first three Spider-Man films, check out "Sam Rami." Go to page 47. ▶▶

of $250 million. Experts at **special effects** began creating enemies for Spider-Man using computer programs.

Special effects made the third *Spider-Man* movie a gem. A construction crane crashes through a skyscraper, putting a woman's life in danger. Later, Spider-Man becomes covered with a sticky black goo that creeps across his body.

Tobey has been praised for his onscreen performances in the *Spider-Man* films. Many people feel that the talented young actor is able to capture Peter Parker's inner doubts and frustrations. At first, however, the company that made the movie was not sure Tobey was the right person for the job. He had to audition for the part several times.

One of the most striking effects was the creation of Sandman. He pulls himself into human form from a pile of sand. The challenge for the special-effects people was to make Sandman look real and amazing at the same time. They had to show him in different forms, from a cloud to a giant. In addition, they had to give the sand creature some personality. As **producer** Grant Curtis notes:

> **We really show the awesome powers that this beast has and how he controls it or doesn't control it.**

➤ A Change in Attitude ◄

Special effects were not the only thing that drew people to the movie. They also wanted to see how Spider-Man changed. The hero had a different look in this movie. As Maguire describes:

> **There is kind of a Goth look to him. The darkness is oozing out of him. He's also got the nerdy version of a cool swagger.**

In *Spider-Man 3*, Spider-Man's superpowers become stronger when he is covered by a black goo that falls from the sky. His new look also brings a change in attitude. He becomes eager for power and revenge. He has to fight with himself in order to choose good over evil.

In addition to an inner conflict, Spider-Man must also battle a number of villains. He fights with his friend Harry, who thinks Spider-Man killed his father. He must deal with Sandman and another new villain named Venom.

Not every reviewer loved the movie. Some said it had too many villains and was confusing. However, Maguire continued to hit his mark as the thoughtful superhero Spider-Man. Reviewer Kevin Lally notes:

> **Maguire somehow still makes us believe in the goofy innocence of Peter Parker.**

As a teen, Maguire knew he wanted to act. "By the time I was sixteen, I felt I had so much inside me," he once said. "I've always known that I have a really powerful spirit and that in life you can have almost anything you want. But you have to be ready to do the things you want to do."

Outcast

THE ACTOR WHO BECAME FAMOUS AS SPIDER-
Man was born on June 27, 1975. Tobias Vincent
Maguire was born in Santa Monica, California. His
mother, Wendy, worked as a secretary. His father,
Vincent Maguire, had jobs as a chef and as a construction worker. When Tobey was born, his mother
was 18 years old and his father was 20.

Tobey's parents were not married when he was born. They got
married after he was born but were divorced before Tobey was two
years old. Tobey has four half brothers.

⇛ MOVING AROUND ⇚

Tobey moved often as a child. He lived with his mother, father, grand-
parents, aunts, and uncles at different times. He lived in California,
Washington, and Oregon, and he was constantly starting over at new
schools. His family was very poor, and he often felt like an outcast.

Moving around was tough on Tobey. He constantly had to make new friends. In sixth grade he prepared to start classes at another new school in Palm Springs. He became so worried that he got sick to his stomach each morning.

➤ TRYING ACTING ◀

Tobey's grandmother taught cooking classes, and he thought of becoming a chef. However, his mother had other ideas. She had wanted to be an actress but gave up that dream after Tobey was born. She encouraged her son to try acting. When he was 12 she gave him $100 to take a drama class. That was an awful lot of money for Tobey, so he gave acting a try. He was surprised to find that he liked it.

By going to many new schools, Tobey learned to watch people. He studied how they behaved. This helped him when it came to acting. He began working as an actor at age 13. First he appeared in commercials. Tobey got his first part on a television program with the 1989 special *Rodney Dangerfield: Opening Night at Rodney's Place.* He only had one line, but he and his mom were excited to go to Las Vegas for the filming of the show. They got to stay in a fancy hotel room and eat for free. They were each paid $50. Tobey loved it:

> **❝**It was so exciting, everything was larger than life. **❞**

CROSS-CURRENTS

Read "Rodney Dangerfield" to learn more about the comedian whose 1989 television special helped launch Tobey's acting career. Go to page 48. ▶▶

➤ SUCCESS ON TELEVISION ◀

In ninth grade Tobey left regular high school to concentrate on his career. He studied videos of Al Pacino, Dustin Hoffman, and Robert De Niro to learn more about acting. He continued to **audition** and got a number of small roles in television series. When he got a speaking part in an **episode** of the **sitcom** *Blossom*, he was quite proud:

> **❝**I was so excited. I had one line and my back was to the camera. I couldn't have been more thrilled. **❞**

Most of Tobey's roles were small ones, but he eventually got a starring role in the show *Great Scott!* The TV series was canceled after nine weeks, but Tobey did get noticed for his work on it. In 1993 he was **nominated** for a Young Artist Award for Best Young Actor in a New Television Series.

≫ UNDER PRESSURE ≪

Although he had some success with small roles, Tobey was also turned down for many parts. He auditioned for the television show *Wonder Years* almost a dozen times but did not get a part. He read for a role in the movie *This Boy's Life* with Robert De Niro, but he did a terrible job.

Comedian Rodney Dangerfield became well known in the 1970s and 1980s. One of the most famous lines from his comedy shows was, "I can't get no respect." As a young teenager, Tobey Maguire had a very small part at the beginning of the 1989 television special, *Rodney Dangerfield: Opening Night at Rodney's Place*.

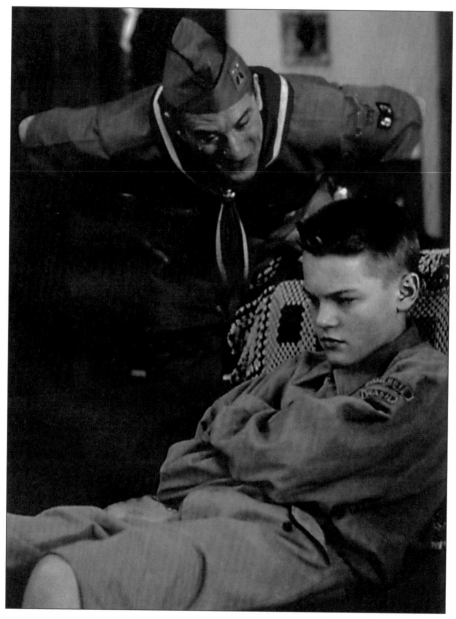

Tobey auditioned for the lead role in *This Boy's Life*, but did not earn the part. Instead, good friend Leonardo DiCaprio won the starring role. Leonardo (right, in a scene from the film) helped Tobey get a small part in the 1993 film. Tobey was excited to work with legendary actor Robert De Niro (standing), one of his heroes.

Losing so many roles was tough on Tobey. One bright spot was his friendship with actor Leonardo DiCaprio. They were both child actors and had become friends. When Leonardo got the role in *This Boy's Life*, he made sure Tobey had a small part in the picture.

CROSS-CURRENTS

If you would like to learn more about Tobey Maguire's actor pal, check out "Leonardo DiCaprio." Go to page 48. ▶▶

Tobey was happy to have even a small role in a movie with Robert De Niro. He had high hopes for himself as an actor. He put a great deal of pressure on himself to succeed.

The pressure began to wear on Tobey as he continued to be rejected for parts. He badly wanted to succeed. His career was not going as well as he wanted it to. By age 18, he began drinking to cope with the pressure.

➤ TURNING THINGS AROUND ◀

Things began to fall apart for Maguire on the set of the movie *Empire Records*. He got a small part in the film but felt like an outcast on the set. He begged to be let out of his contract, and the **director** agreed.

After Maguire left the movie he took time to think about his life. He considered his attitude toward work. He realized he could not continue to push himself so hard.

Maguire came up with a new way of looking at his career. He would accept stardom if it came, but he would be fine if it did not. He saw there was more to life than being famous.

At age 19, Maguire entered Alcoholics Anonymous and quit drinking alcohol. He began to take care of himself. He became a vegetarian and began practicing yoga. He says,

> **❝ I had to make a decision: I could be a teenager and do all the stupid things that go along with that or focus on acting. Instead of going out and getting drunk, I ended up staying home and reading scripts. ❞**

Tobey took some time away from acting. He did not go to auditions for six months. When he returned to the career he loved, it was with a new attitude. He was not looking for fame, but he was ready to do his best and find roles that interested him.

Putting his acting career on hold when he was 19 helped Tobey to understand himself and to become a better actor. "It all came from my values switching and not being so desperate to be successful," he later said. "I just kind of went, 'If [success] comes, it comes, but that's not what life is about.'"

Respected Actor

TOBEY MAGUIRE REMAINED SERIOUS ABOUT acting and carefully considered roles that came his way, but he also changed his attitude about the importance of success. This new approach worked. Once Tobey took the pressure off himself to succeed, he began getting larger roles and receiving greater attention for his talent.

One of his first starring roles was in the 1996 movie *Joyride*. The film was about a group of teens who steal a car and find a dead body in the trunk. The film got terrible reviews, but before long Maguire was chosen for a short movie that was much more respected.

Maguire had a starring role in the well-regarded short film *The Duke of Groove*. He played a nerdy teen, and actress Kate Capshaw played his mother. The movie included appearances by a number of big-name actors, including Keifer Sutherland and Elliot Gould.

CROSS-CURRENTS

To learn more about actress Kate Capshaw, an early mentor for Tobey, check out "Kate Capshaw." Go to page 50. ▶▶

The movie showed a strong relationship between a mother and son, and in real life Capshaw became supportive of Maguire. She helped him gain confidence and look at life in a new way. Maguire's new attitude helped his performance shine. The film was nominated for an Oscar. Directors began to notice Maguire, and he soon found himself in demand.

⟫ IN THE GROOVE ⟪

One of the people who admired Maguire's performance in *The Duke of Groove* was director Ang Lee. He was making a movie about a troubled family and wanted Maguire to be part of it. The movie was *The Ice Storm*, and Maguire got a role as a lonely, sensitive teen, a part he understood well.

Maguire's career edged up a notch with *The Ice Storm*. The movie starred Sigourney Weaver and Oscar-winning actor Kevin Kline. The 21-year-old Maguire had an important scene early in the movie that set a thoughtful and fateful tone for the tragedy.

Maguire received some good news while he was on the set of the film. He learned that director Woody Allen wanted him to be in his next movie, the 1997 film *Deconstructing Harry*. Maguire was thrilled to work with such a well-known director. He was making his mark playing teens who were filled with anxiety, but he could not have been happier. As Maguire states,

"I happen to be blessed. People keep themselves unhappy. I see the world as a big huge playground that I get to enjoy."

CROSS-CURRENTS

If you would like more information about the award-winning director of Deconstructing Harry, read "Woody Allen." Go to page 50. ▶▶

⟫ LEADING MAN ⟪

Maguire's role in *Deconstructing Harry* was a small one. The movie starred Allen as an author named Harry. The film had a large cast and featured a number of stars, from Robin Williams to Billy Crystal. Maguire had a part as one of Harry's book characters.

Maguire's next movie role was also a minor part. He played a hitchhiker in the 1998 movie *Fear and Loathing in Las Vegas*. That movie starred Johnny Depp, but the young Maguire was gaining respect. Maguire was soon on his way to starring roles as well.

A scene from *The Ice Storm*, a 1994 film by director Ang Lee. The movie about two troubled families living in Connecticut during the early 1970s featured a number of established stars, including Kevin Kline and Sigourney Weaver. Tobey (second from left) costarred with several other up-and-coming actors, including Christina Ricci and Elijah Wood.

Maguire had his first leading role in a major movie that year. The film was *Pleasantville*, directed by Gary Ross. Maguire and Reese Witherspoon played a brother and sister who become trapped in a 1950s television sitcom. The world they are taken to is too perfect to be true. They shake up Pleasantville with their thoughts and ideas. Maguire plays a teen who is at first awed by this new world. Reviewer Lisa Schwarzbaum liked his style. After describing a scene in which Maguire marvels at what he sees, she comments,

> **"Maguire, with his sweet, smart-kid grin, is an excellent marveler."**

Maguire's performance in *Pleasantville* earned him a Saturn Award for Best Performance by a Younger Actor/Actress. His work also impressed the director. Ross would remember Maguire when it came time to make the movie *Seabiscuit*.

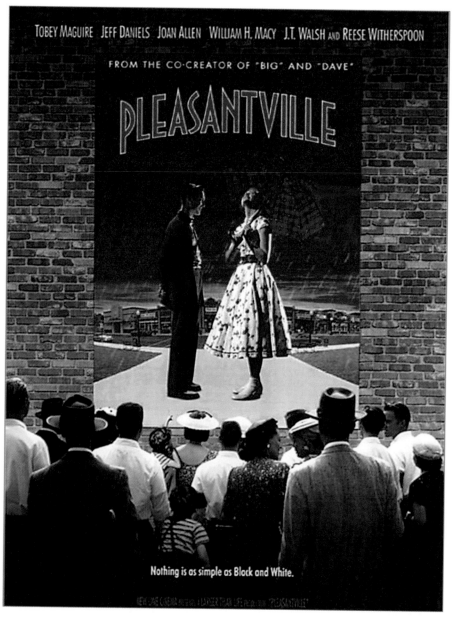

In the 1998 film *Pleasantville*, two modern-day teenagers (played by Tobey and Reese Witherspoon) are transported into the idyllic world of a 1950s television show. The film was praised for its interesting technique. Director Gary Ross combined black-and-white images with color shots to represent changes that occur in the lives of the characters.

≫ WELL-CHOSEN ROLES ≪

Ross was not the only director who enjoyed working with Maguire. Director Ang Lee had also been was struck by his talent, and he chose Maguire to be in the Civil War drama *Ride with the Devil*. The movie is about a group of soldiers fighting on the Kansas and Missouri border. Maguire played Jake, a 19-year-old boy who decides to fight for the South after his friend's father is killed by the Yankees. His youthful character is tested by the pain of war.

The movie did not make a great deal of money. However, the role of Jake was one that Maguire found interesting. He wanted to build his career by choosing his roles wisely. He realized that he did not have a great deal of control over whether a movie made money:

> **CROSS-CURRENTS**
> Read "Ang Lee" if you would like to learn more about the acclaimed director of "Ride with the Devil." Go to page 51. ▶▶

> **❝For me personally, the results aren't exactly in my hands. All I can do is choose films, and hopefully, good ones come my way.❞**

≫ POSITIVE REVIEWS ≪

Maguire's next movie was a successful one. He had a large role in the 1999 film *The Cider House Rules*, which was nominated for a best-picture Oscar. The movie tells the story of a doctor who works at an orphanage in Maine, and the young man who helps him there. Maguire was chosen for the movie after director Lasse Hallstrom was impressed by his performance in *The Ice Storm*.

Maguire played a quiet, sensitive character who learns some tough lessons about life. His costar in the movie was Michael Caine, who received a supporting-actor Oscar for his work. The movie cast was also nominated for a Kids' Choice Award and a Teen Choice Award. For his performance, Maguire received kind words from movie reviewers. In *Entertainment Weekly*, Lisa Schwarzbaum said,

> **❝Maguire acquires a new, leaner maturity. The 24-year-old . . . is one of the most natural young actors working today.❞**

➤ A CAPTIVATING ACTOR ◄

Maguire also received good reviews for his role in his next movie, *Wonder Boys*, directed by Curtis Hanson. The movie starred Michael Douglas as a college professor who is being pressured to complete a book and is also dealing with a failed marriage and an affair. Maguire played a thoughtful young college student who has an angry side. It was a disturbing character, but Maguire made him fascinating. Reviewer Peter Travers says Maguire's character in this movie was

"captivating and creepy in equal doses."

Maguire's performance was an award-winning one. He received a Toronto Film Critics Association Award for Best Supporting Performance, Male, for his work in *Wonder Boys*. Movie **critic** Owen Gleiberman says Maguire has the ability to pull off a complicated role:

"This young actor was born to play cerebral misfits—with his baby-owl stare, he keeps you focused on what he's not saying."

Maguire was a powerful actor, but he knew how to deliver a strong performance without overwhelming the audience. He had learned to control his emotions long ago, as a child constantly moving and attending new schools. Now he impressed audiences and critics alike by delivering a strong performance in a subtle way.

Maguire's strength was his ability to convey emotion without overdoing it. He could get messages about his character's thoughts across by the way he moved his eyes. A tiny movement of his mouth could deliver a message about what his character was feeling. Hanson, the *Wonder Boys* director, noticed this about the young actor:

"One of the things that distinguishes Tobey as an actor is his ability to do more while appearing to do less."

➤ A HARD WORKER ◄

Maguire's acting ability did not come easily, however. He worked hard at finding different ways to get his character's thoughts and

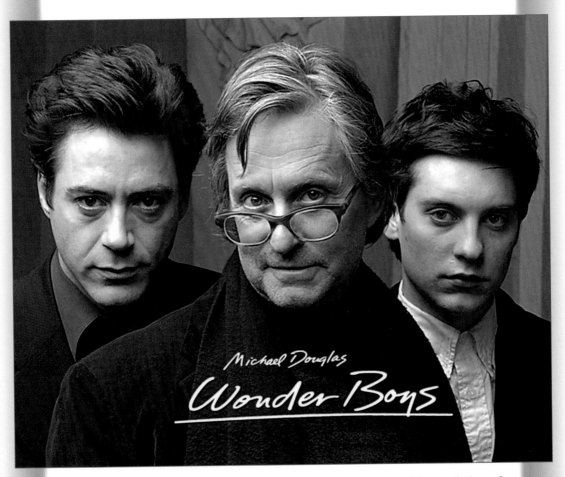

Michael Douglas
Wonder Boys

In the 2000 film *Wonder Boys*, Tobey starred with acclaimed actors Michael Douglas (center) and Robert Downey Jr. (left). The film was a flop at the box office. However, Tobey's strong performance received good reviews from movie critics. Tobey also won an award from the Toronto Film Critics Association for his acting in *Wonder Boys*.

feelings to come through. He knew he was working with some of the best actors and directors in the business. The young actor did not want to disappointment them:

> **"I'm really with the pros. I wouldn't think of arriving on the set without being on time, knowing my lines, and having 10 different ways to play the scene."**

TOBEY MAGUIRE

Maguire carefully chose the parts he played and the people he worked with. He wanted to work with people he could learn from. His goal was to improve as an actor, not just appear on a movie screen.

Maguire was known for playing thoughtful, sensitive characters. He played those parts well, but he knew he could do even more. He

After starring roles in *The Cider House Rules*, *Ride with the Devil*, and *Wonder Boys*, Tobey Maguire was recognized as one of America's top young actors. He decided to take a short break from making films, but it wasn't long until a great role came along: as the main character in *Spider-Man*.

had not yet shown all of his acting skills onscreen, and he was happy to have even more to offer in future movies:

> **"I can be pretty subtle and do my thing, but I love to pop out of that. I'm excited that people have only seen so much of me, because then I get to surprise people. And that's the best part."**

➤ TAKING A BREAK ⬅

Maguire's roles in *Ride with the Devil*, *The Cider House Rules*, and *Wonder Boys* had all been parts that had captured his interest. He had enjoyed making the movies, but he found that his busy schedule was wearing on him. The movies were all released in 1999, and Maguire had worked for 18 months straight. He had not wanted to turn down any great roles, but he was tired after working for so long.

Maguire decided he needed to stop making movies for a time. He was exhausted and needed a break. He wanted to settle down at home rather than head off to another movie set. He wanted to cook dinners for his friends and just relax.

He realized that leaving movies for a while could hurt his career. Actors who take themselves out of the public eye risk being forgotten. Maguire was willing to take this chance. He did not want to stop acting forever, but he strongly felt that he needed some time off to reenergize. He was confident that his career could withstand a little down time:

> **"I have faith that nothing will be lost by relaxing. I act as if I have all the opportunities in the world. People around me think I'm crazy, but I just have faith that the right stuff will come to me."**

Maguire did not give up on acting, but he wanted to wait until the right role came along before taking on another movie. He spent some time playing basketball and poker. He also read scripts. It would take something well written and different to bring him back to the movie screen. Maguire found it when he read the script for *Spider-Man*.

Once he landed the role of Spider-Man, Tobey exercised to build up his muscles. He also trained to become more flexible and learned how to move gracefully. Tobey's hard work paid off, as *Spider-Man* became the biggest hit of 2002. The film eventually earned more than $800 million in theaters worldwide.

Superstar

SPIDER-MAN WAS A DIFFERENT KIND OF ACTION hero, and director Sam Raimi thought Maguire was the perfect actor to take on the role. He had seen him in *The Cider House Rules* and had been impressed. He thought Maguire had the right look and talent for the part of Spider-Man.

Maguire also had respect for Raimi's work. Raimi had directed movies from horror films and thrillers to dramas, often adding a touch of humor to them. Maguire did not want to play Spider-Man as only a forceful superhero. The role appealed to him because Spider-Man was about more than action. According to Maguire,

> **"**Spider-Man for me is such a great character because he's so relatable. I mean, he's a regular kid who gets these super powers and he can relate to them as a human being. Then, he's also a super-hero, but even being a superhero, he's conflicted like a human being would be.**"**

➤ FIGHTING TO BE SPIDER-MAN ◀

Not everyone agreed that Maguire was right for the part. He had earned a reputation for playing sensitive, serious characters in low-budget movies. Although the movies were praised by critics, they did not often bring in a great deal of money at the box office. By contrast, *Spider-Man* was a high-profile action movie about a comic-book character. It had a huge budget. Maguire had never made a film like this before.

In addition, there was concern over Maguire's popularity. Some movie studio executives thought an actor who was more of teen heartthrob should take the role. They also wanted someone who proved he could bring in big money at the box office. Actors such as Freddie Prinze Jr., Heath Ledger, and Leonardo DiCaprio all tried out for the part of Spider-Man.

Raimi still liked Maguire for the part, however. He wanted someone who looked young enough to play Spider-Man at age 17. He also wanted someone with a slight, strong build. In addition, the actor had to show the sensitive side of the superhero. Maguire had those qualities and more, Raimi says:

> **"He's got magnetism. He's subtle and quite powerful in his stillness. "**

➤ EARNING THE PART ◀

To make sure that Maguire was the right person for the job, he was asked to two screen tests. He had to do a love scene as well as an action scene. He proved that he could handle both. He was offered the part and was eager to prove that the director had made the right choice. Maguire comments,

> **"I look forward to constantly changing people's opinions of me. I think that's the fun of it. "**

To get into shape for the part, Maguire trained hard for five months. He needed to be strong and agile to play the nimble superhero. To prepare for the role, he trained twice a day, six days per week. He worked out with a martial-arts instructor. He also learned gymnastics moves, worked with a yoga trainer, and did weight training.

Director Sam Raimi (right) admitted being a fan of the comic-book superhero from a young age. "As a child, the thing that drew me to Spider-Man wasn't just watching Peter become a hero and identifying with that, but also identifying with his desire to be noticed," Raimi said. "The human story has always been the strength of the comic."

⟫ FANS CAUGHT IN THE WEB ⟪

Spider-Man was a hit with audiences as soon as it spun into theaters in 2002. It broke a record by bringing in $114 million in its first weekend. By the next weekend it had earned more than $200 million.

Fans were drawn to the comedy, romance, and action of the film. Maguire drew laughs as he played Peter Parker learning to use his web-spinning and leaping powers. He gained credibility as a romantic hero with an upside-down kiss with costar Kirsten Dunst, who played Mary Jane. His battle with the Green Goblin, played by Willem Dafoe, gave the movie a thrilling action scene.

CROSS-CURRENTS

To find out more about the life of one of Tobey's Spider-Man costars, check out "Kirsten Dunst." Go to page 52. ▶▶

Peter Parker begins to learn about his amazing powers in a scene from *Spider-Man*. Columbia Pictures paid Tobey Maguire $4 million to play Parker, the young man who becomes a superhero. However, as part of the deal, Tobey had to agree to appear in two sequels if the first film was a success.

In addition, Maguire captured Spider-Man's inner turmoil. He showed how the hero learns to use his powers for the benefit of others rather than himself. He was praised for the way he captured the personality of Peter Parker.

The movie eventually brought in more than $800 million worldwide and took Maguire's career to the level of superstardom. He had proven he could make a blockbuster film and be a movie hero. In addition, two sequels were planned, assuring the actor of steady work in movies that were almost certain to be successful. Maguire's life had been forever changed by Spider-Man.

⇒ SPIDEY'S IMPACT ⇐

After *Spider-Man* was released, Maguire also had to deal with the more difficult side of fame. Photographers began to follow him, hoping to get a shot of the star. On the weekend that *Spider-Man* came out, a dozen were waiting for him in the parking lot after he left a restaurant. More were waiting for him at home. He tried not to let it bother him, however, and tried to go about his life as he always had.

Maguire also managed his career the same way he had before. He had built his career by being choosy about the films he was in. By age 28 he had worked with a series of talented directors. He had made $4 million for *Spider-Man*, and he knew the value of choosing roles carefully:

> **"I wait. I don't want to work as an actor just because I haven't worked in six months. I want to only do things when I really want to do them, and if they only come along every year, year and a half, then that's fine."**

➤ A NEW ROLE ◀

Maguire took on more responsibility for his next movies. In addition to acting, he also took on the role of producer. This gave him the ability to have more say in how the movie was made and who appeared in it. Maguire explains,

> **"It's very much as time allows, but I want to be involved at every level. I'm just dipping my feet in, but I want to make some good films. I'm looking for things to develop, both with me as a producer and an actor."**

He began his work as a producer on the movie *25th Hour*, directed by Spike Lee. The 2002 film followed a man on the day before he was sent to prison. Maguire also planned to star in the film, but he had to drop out when he was offered a part in the movie *Seabiscuit*. Edward Norton took over the role in *25th Hour*, and Maguire went on to act in and produce the movie about a championship horse.

 SEABISCUIT

Maguire was director Gary Ross's first choice to play jockey Red Pollard in *Seabiscuit*. Ross wrote the movie's screenplay and created the part with Maguire in mind. The true story tells how a broken-down horse

The 2003 film *Seabiscuit* was based on a true story about a great racehorse from the 1930s. Tobey (left) played jockey John "Red" Pollard, who develops a strong bond with the horse. The film also starred Chris Cooper (leaning on wall) as trainer Tom Smith, and Jeff Bridges and Elizabeth Banks (right) as the racehorse's owners, Charles and Marcela Howard.

and a bitter jockey become champions together during the Great Depression of the 1930s. Maguire was drawn to the part because it showed how someone who was down and out could succeed:

CROSS-CURRENTS

Read "Gary Ross" to learn more about the life and career of the director of Seabiscuit. Go to page 53. ▶▶

"It's not just about winning a race and beating the odds. It's about overcoming your own emotional and psychological obstacles."

This movie was a test for Maguire. It would show whether audiences would accept him for something other than the Spider-Man role for which he had become so well known. The role marked the first time he played an adult, and it increased his salary to $12.5 million.

THE HEART OF A CHAMPION

Once again, Maguire carefully prepared for the role. Jockeys are slim and light; he had to lose 20 pounds and reduce his body fat to 6 percent. He also spent hours riding a mechanical horse and real horses.

Maguire's efforts were worth it. The heartwarming story was a winner with audiences and movie critics. It made $20 million its first weekend and went on to bring in more than $120 million. When *Seabiscuit* was released in 2003, movie reviewer Peter Travers noted that Maguire played his role with feeling that showed how he and the horse help heal each other.

The movie proved that Maguire could pull in large audiences outside his successful role as Spider-Man. The film made an impact on his personal life as well. While working on the movie in 2003, he met Jennifer Meyer. Meyer was the daughter of Ron Meyer, the head of Universal Studios. She and Maguire soon began a serious relationship.

A HEALTH CONCERN

Maguire's work on *Seabiscuit* helped the movie become successful, but it almost cost him his role as Spider-Man. He injured his back while making *Seabiscuit*, and there was concern that he would not be able to take on the athletic role of the superhero in *Spider-Man 2*.

Actor Jake Gyllenhaal began preparing to take on the role, but Maguire did not give up. He met with the movie executives and director Sam Raimi. He proved that he was fit enough to again play the limber superhero. He was given the part—and a $17 million paycheck.

SPIDEY'S BACK

Maguire's character in *Spider-Man 2* had a different outlook than he had in the original movie. Peter Parker had been awestruck by his powers in the first film. In the second, doubts creep in. Parker struggles with loneliness as he keeps his superhero identity a secret. His heart aches when Mary Jane plans to marry another man. Spider-Man wonders if being a hero is worth giving up a normal life and the woman he loves.

The superhero manages to put his personal concerns aside and battle a new villain, Dr. Otto Octavius. He wins Mary Jane's heart and saves her, as well as a train loaded with strong-hearted New Yorkers, from the evil Doc Ock. Maguire once again captured the humor and drama of his character. His work on the movie earned him a Saturn Award for best actor as well as a nomination for an Empire Award and Kids' Choice Award. Reviewer Lisa Schwarzbaum gives the *Spider-Man* sequel an A:

Tobey poses with girlfriend Jennifer Meyer at a movie premiere. The two met when Tobey was working on *Seabiscuit*, and soon began dating. Jennifer, who is two years younger than Tobey, has worked in the fashion industry. She currently owns a jewelry business and designs necklaces, earrings, rings, and bracelets.

Spider-Man battles Doctor Octopus in a scene from *Spider-Man* 2. Many people liked the second film in the series better than the first. In *Spider-Man* 2, Peter Parker considers giving up his secret life as a crime-fighting superhero. However, Peter eventually realizes that he has a responsibility to use his super powers to help others.

> **"**When he doubts himself, Spidey finds that his spinning goo clogs up and becomes unreliable. But when he's happy, he sticks his landings perfectly. So does this movie. **"**

The movie was a resounding success. It brought in $88 million on its opening weekend and went on to earn almost $800 million worldwide. Now audiences waited to see if Maguire would follow it up with another thrilling performance in *Spider-Man 3*.

Tobey Maguire smiles during a New York event to promote one of his films. Now that he has established himself as a top young actor, Tobey has begun to branch into other areas of the entertainment business, such as producing films. He also keeps busy by doing things with his family.

5

Fame and Family

MAGUIRE'S CAREER WAS SOARING. HE WAS praised for his work in *Spider-Man 2* and was set to make $17 million for *Spider-Man 3*. He had never been so popular. He was admired for his talent and for the way he lived his life. He had overcome a difficult childhood and had turned away from drinking and other harmful behavior.

He continued to take care of himself while supporting the people and causes that mattered to him. He continued to be a vegetarian and practiced yoga to keep himself in shape. Concerned about the humane treatment of animals, he did not allow people to wear leather in his home. He supported voter education and contributed to Lifebeat, the music industry's AIDS fund-raising and service charity.

CROSS-CURRENTS

If you want to know more about an ancient discipline Tobey practices to stay in shape, read "Yoga." Go to page 54. ▶▶

⋙ A NEW FAMILY ⋘

As his career continued on an upward path, Maguire's personal life began reaching a new high as well. He continued his relationship with Jennifer Meyer. They became engaged in April 2006. Meyer was thrilled to be part of Maguire's life:

> **"**Let's just say this is truly the best time of my life. I'm walking on air.**"**

The couple's first child was born on November 10, 2006. They named the little girl Ruby Sweetheart. The name was chosen in honor of Meyer's grandmother, who liked to call Meyer by the nickname "Sweetheart."

Maguire and Meyer got married in a ceremony in Hawaii on September 4, 2007. Friends and relatives attended the ceremony, including Maguire's good friend Leonardo DiCaprio.

⋙ A NEW DIRECTION ⋘

While his personal life was going smoothly in 2006, Maguire's professional one hit a minor bump. Maguire planned to make another *Spider-Man* movie, but first he had a different type of film in mind. He did not want to get **typecast** as a superhero. Before he began making *Spider-Man 3* he went in a new direction. For his next project, he chose a movie set in the 1940s.

Maguire worked with actor George Clooney and director Steven Soderbergh in the movie *The Good German.* Clooney starred in the movie as a journalist who is working in Berlin, Germany, at the end of World War II. Clooney's character is also looking for a woman he had met before the war.

Maguire had a supporting role in the film, which was released in 2006. He played the soldier assigned to be Clooney's driver. This character was miles away from the superhero he had become famous for playing. Maguire's character, Patrick Tully, was dishonest and shady. He thought only of himself, and he did not care whom he hurt in the process.

The movie was much more dark and dramatic than the flashy *Spider-Man* movies. The drama movie turned into a mystery when Maguire's character was killed and Clooney tried to find out who had committed the murder.

Soderbergh tried to make the movie appear as if it had been made in the 1940s. He used footage and a camera from that era. The end product was not well received, however. Critics said the movie was confusing and the 1940s style did not work well. Reviewer Todd McCarthy notes,

> "Steven Soderbergh tries to make one like they used to and comes up short with *The Good German*."

The Good German was one of Maguire's few failures. Reviewers said he was miscast as the underhanded driver. He was also

In the 2006 film *The Good German*, Tobey (left) starred with George Clooney (center) and Cate Blanchett (right). Tobey's character, a murdered American soldier who had been involved in illegal business dealings, was unlike his usual good-guy characters. However, the black-and-white film received mixed reviews from movie critics and did not earn much money.

criticized for failing to connect with Clooney's character. The movie allowed him to step away from his good-guy roles, but it did not earn him admiration.

⇒ READY FOR *SPIDER-MAN* ⇐

The unsuccessful movie was a minor film compared to the wildly popular *Spider-Man* series. Maguire was soon back on track to release another movie in the series. He prepared to start shooting the movie, and he was set to earn $17 million to take on the role.

Maguire once again set about earning the respect he had received for the role. He worked out to get in shape for the movie. He worked with a trainer and did Pilates and yoga exercises. He also used boxing and biking to get into shape.

Maguire worked out so he would have the muscles that made him look the part of Spider-Man, but he admitted that he did not do all his stunts in the movie. His back felt fine, and he did some of the stunts himself, but he said that stunt men took over for the more difficult feats:

> **"I do the stuff that I can do and that is safe. When I watch the stuntmen do the really, really crazy stuff it blows my mind and I say, 'I can't believe they do that.' It's really amazing . . . any actor that says they do all their stunts is not telling you the truth! Unless they are like, jumping over a little gate or something. "**

⇒ A NEW TWIST FOR SPIDEY ⇐

This was the third time Maguire would play the same character, but he said he did not tire of playing Spider-Man. He found the third film to have more interesting twists than the first two did. Maguire's challenge was to show how Spider-Man was changing yet remain true to his personality:

> **"It is important to not just try to create new things for Peter just for the sake of it, but I don't necessarily want to see the same scenes played out and Peter going through the same kind of things that he has gone through. As an actor**

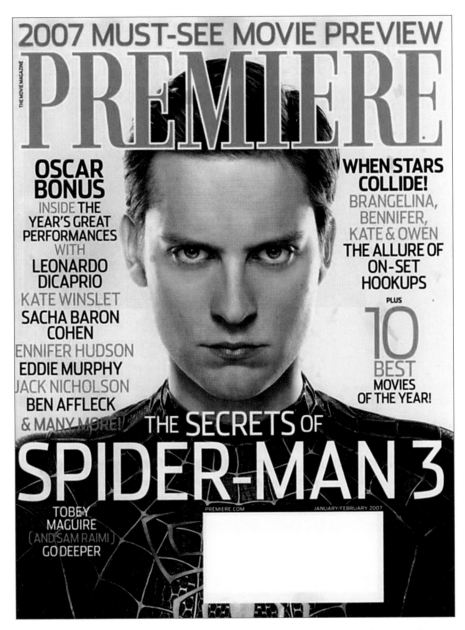

2007 MUST-SEE MOVIE PREVIEW

PREMIERE

THE MOVIE MAGAZINE

OSCAR BONUS

INSIDE THE YEAR'S GREAT PERFORMANCES WITH

LEONARDO DICAPRIO

KATE WINSLET

SACHA BARON COHEN

ENNIFER HUDSON

EDDIE MURPHY

JACK NICHOLSON

BEN AFFLECK

& MANY MORE!

WHEN STARS COLLIDE!

BRANGELINA, BENNIFER, KATE & OWEN

THE ALLURE OF ON-SET HOOKUPS

PLUS

10 BEST MOVIES OF THE YEAR!

THE SECRETS OF SPIDER-MAN 3

TOBEY MAGUIRE (AND SAM RAIMI) GO DEEPER

PREMIERE.COM   JANUARY/FEBRUARY 2007

Wearing his new black costume, Tobey was pictured on the cover of *Premiere* magazine's January/February 2007 issue. *Spider-Man 3* was a huge international hit when it was released in May of that year. It set a record for the most money earned by a film during its first weekend in theaters.

In *Spider-Man 3*, Tobey Maguire's superhero character battles a number of enemies, including the shape-shifting Sandman, the New Goblin, and the alien Venom. However, in the film Peter Parker must also confront the good and bad within himself. This is his toughest challenge, but Parker proves to be up to the task.

there is nothing stale about it. I got to approach it and got to do brand new and interesting things for myself. **"**

In *Spider-Man 3*, Maguire took the character to another level. Far from being insecure, Peter Parker is now overconfident, although in a nerdy type of way. He struts and becomes cocky. He even shares an upside-down kiss with a beautiful blonde who is not his girlfriend, Mary Jane. To make matters worse, a black goo brings out his angry side and threatens to overtake him.

In addition to dealing with the anger inside himself, Spider-Man has to take on three villains. He fights with his friend Harry, who is angry with Spider-Man because of his father's death. He also battles Flint Marko, who transforms into Sandman. In addition, a rival photographer at the newspaper turns into the evil Venom.

≫ TANGLED WEB ≪

These villains and plotlines were a lot to fit into a movie that lasted a little over two hours. Some reviewers thought *Spider-Man 3* tried to do too much and became confusing. However, audiences loved the film, and it was nominated for several Teen Choice Awards. It broke opening-day records by bringing in $60 million. Audiences apparently agreed with critic David Ansen, who said,

> **"Somehow this ambitious mishmash works. It's both the most grandiose chapter and the nuttiest."**

Spider-Man remained a wildly popular character, and Maguire again earned praise for the way he portrayed the superhero. However, the actor did not commit to making a fourth *Spider-Man* movie. As Maguire explains,

> **"It's hard to imagine continuously coming up with stories that deserve to be told. I'm not sure if there are more stories for this character that are interesting enough to be excited about doing more."**

≫ STAYING BUSY ≪

While Maguire was not sure if he would again play Spider-Man, there was no doubt he would continue to act and produce. The actor was busier than ever after he finished making and promoting *Spider-Man 3*. The success of the *Spider-Man* films put him in a position to have a hand in creating the movies he wanted to make.

Maguire had worked as a producer on *Seabiscuit* and on the television show *Rock of Ages*. He took his career as a producer in a new direction when he planned to bring *Robotech* to the screen. *Robotech* would be a science-fiction movie based on a 1980s cartoon series from Japan. The series featured giant robots from outer space who fend off aliens.

A celebrity photographer snapped this photo of Tobey holding his infant daughter Ruby Sweetheart while walking with wife Jennifer Meyer. Jennifer and Tobey were married in a secret ceremony in Hawaii on September 3, 2007. Although he remains in demand as an actor, Tobey has told the media that he prefers spending time with his family.

The movie would be produced through Maguire Entertainment, and Maguire also planned to play the lead role. He said the storyline had a strong foundation, and that it offered the chance to make an entertaining movie.

In addition to *Robotech*, Maguire also prepared to produce and act in the movie *Tokyo Suckerpunch*. The movie is about a writer who travels to Japan and is surprised by what he finds there. It was directed by his friend Gary Ross, who had also directed him in *Seabiscuit* and *Pleasantville*.

CROSS-CURRENTS

To find out more about star actors who have gotten involved in the production of Hollywood movies, read "Actors/Producers." Go to page 54. ▶▶

Maguire also signed on to make the movie *Quiet Type* and was part of the cast of the movie *Brothers*. *Brothers* also stars Natalie Portman and Jake Gyllenhaal and tells the story of a family impacted by the war in Afghanistan.

In 2008 Maguire also had a role in a movie that spoofed war films. Ben Stiller brought together a large cast for the film *Tropic Thunder*, and Maguire was part of the comedy. On the production side, Maguire teamed up with producer Neal Moritz for another science-fiction movie. The adventure set in the future would be a movie version of the comic book *Afterburn*.

≫ FAMILY FIRST ≪

Maguire was in the middle of a number of different projects in 2008 as well. He was looking forward to trying new things as both a producer and an actor. Spider-Man had been his most successful role to this point, but it would certainly not be his last.

In the midst of his busy, successful career, Maguire also found time to spend with his family. He and his wife bought a site for a new home in the Brentwood section of Los Angeles. They also spent time with their daughter, taking her to the park and pushing her on the swing. In public, he gave the little girl hugs and kisses and showered her with attention.

Tobey Maguire has come a long way from the lonely child who hid his emotions and grew tired of making friends. He has a beautiful daughter and a loving wife. He is a respected actor with an interesting career and a happy family life. Even a superhero could not ask for more.

Spider-Man's Enemies

With each new installment in the movie series, Spider-Man faces another evildoer. The superpowers of his enemies often are the result of science experiments gone awry. Here is a look at the villains that Spider-Man has battled in the first three films:

Spider-Man:

The Green Goblin: Norman Osborn is a businessman who is under pressure to develop a new formula for the military. It is supposed to make soldiers stronger, but something goes wrong with the formula. When Osborn tries the formula on himself, it gives him super strength but drives him insane. Riding on a glider and throwing balls of flames, he becomes the Green Goblin and the enemy of Spider-Man.

Spider-Man 2:

Dr. Otto Octavius: A research scientist, Dr. Octavius has invented a set of mechanical arms in order to help him perform an experiment. When something goes terribly wrong, the arms become part of his body and begin to control his mind. Octavius is determined to finish his experiment and battles Spider-Man as he tries to do so.

Spider-Man 3:

Sandman: Flint Marko escapes from prison and stumbles into a science experiment. It turns him into The Sandman, a creature who can shift shapes. He can grow to an enormous height or become a sand cloud. He has no problem pulling himself back together after he is punched or pushed against a moving train. Peter Parker learns that Flint Marko was the man who killed his Uncle Ben (this occurred in the first film), and he sets out to get revenge.

Venom: Eddie Brock Jr. is a new photographer at the *Daily Bugle*. He becomes Peter Parker's rival at the paper and creates a fake picture of Spider-Man. He becomes covered with a black goo and turns into Venom. He looks like an evil version of Spider-Man, with fangs and an all-black suit, and he becomes strong and agile.

The New Goblin: Harry Osborn, Peter Parker's good friend, stumbles upon his father's Green Goblin costume. He blames Spider-Man for his father's death and, out for revenge, he tracks down Spider-Man.

Himself: Spider-Man becomes covered with a black goo that drops from outer space. It makes him stronger, but it also increases his feelings of anger. He must fight his new hunger for power.

(Go back to page 6.)

Sam Raimi

Director Sam Raimi has worked on television shows, horror films, and blockbusters. A native of Detroit, Michigan, he loves the *Spider-Man* comic books. When he met with movie-studio executives to talk about directing *Spider-Man*, he impressed them with his passion.

Raimi began making movies as a child. Using his father's camera, he and some friends made films about the Civil War and other events. He got his start as a professional director by making a movie with some friends. They left college at Michigan State University to make *The Evil Dead*. The movie featured students attacked by zombies. Raimi had a hard time getting the movie shown in the United States, but it became a hit in Europe. His work on the movie led to other horror films. He also directed the *Darkman* movies and was a producer for the television series *Xena: Warrior Princess*.

In 2001 he got the job of directing *Spider-Man*. Raimi wanted to make Spider-Man fans happy with the movie and did it by following his instincts:

> **"I finally told myself that the best way to please the fans is [to] not necessarily listen to them, but to follow in my heart what I love about the comic book and bring that to the screen."**

(Go back to page 8.)

Director Sam Raimi (right) during the filming of Spider-Man 2*. His three films about the comic-book superhero have been extremely successful, earning more than $2.4 billion at the box office. Some of Raimi's other movies include* The Evil Dead *(1981),* Darkman *(1990),* The Quick and the Dead *(1995),* For Love of the Game *(1999), and* The Gift *(2000).*

Rodney Dangerfield

One of the first roles Tobey Maguire landed was in a television special featuring comedian Rodney Dangerfield. Dangerfield took on the role of a down-and-out comedian and was known for the line, "I don't get no respect."

Dangerfield, who was born in 1921, launched his comedy career while he was a teenager. He left show business for the more stable job of selling house paint and siding, but he never stopped writing jokes. He returned to show business in 1962, and in the 1970s he opened the comedy club Dangerfield's in Manhattan. Many unknown comedians got their start at his club, including Jim Carrey, Jerry Seinfeld, and Adam Sandler.

Dangerfield performed at his comedy club and occasionally appeared on *The Tonight Show*. A part in the 1980 comedy film *Caddyshack* brought him greater attention and roles in other movies, such as *Easy Money* and *Back to School*. He also had a dramatic role in the movie *Natural Born Killers* and made a number of television specials for HBO.

Dangerfield released a number of comedy albums during his career and published his autobiography in 2004. Although he suffered from heart problems, he continued to perform. Dangerfield died after having heart surgery in 2004.

(Go back to page 12.)

Leonardo DiCaprio

Like Tobey Maguire, Leonardo DiCaprio got his start as a child actor. Leonardo and Tobey often saw each other at auditions, and they became friends. Leonardo had success at an earlier age than Tobey, however.

DiCaprio was born in 1974 and grew up on a poor side of Los Angeles. He began acting in 1990, with a role on the television series *Parenthood*. His career continued as he got parts in commercials and more small roles on television shows. In 1991 he became part of the cast of the television series *Growing Pains*.

In 1993 DiCaprio won a leading role in the movie *This Boy's Life* opposite Robert

De Niro. He earned praise for this role, as well as for playing a mentally impaired teen in *What's Eating Gilbert Grape?*

DiCaprio appeared in *The Basketball Diaries* and in *Romeo+Juliet* before becoming a superstar and teen heartthrob with the movie *Titanic*. DiCaprio starred as Jack Dawson, a young artist who romances a wealthy socialite named Rose (played by Kate Winslet) on the ill-fated cruise. The movie broke box-office records when it was released in 1997, bringing in more than $1.8 billion.

Titanic made DiCaprio a superstar. Many critics admired his confident portrayal of

A promotional poster for the 1997 motion picture Titanic, *which made Tobey's friend Leonardo DiCaprio an international superstar. Tobey and Leo met when both were young actors going on auditions in the early 1990s. "Watching Leo was great for me because he's really good and I respect him as an actor," Tobey admitted in a 1998 interview.*

Dawson. His salary shot up to $20 million per picture, and he made it a point to choose more adventurous projects.

His follow-up movie, *The Beach*, was not as well received, but he redeemed himself with strong performances in the movies *Gangs of New York* and *Catch Me if You Can*. The actor has earned $20 million per picture for films such as *Blood Diamond* and *The Departed*, both released in 2006, and the 2004 movie *The Aviator*.

One of the people impressed by the actor is director Martin Scorsese, who worked with DiCaprio on *Gangs of New York*. Scorsese says of DiCaprio,

> **"He holds the screen, like a great silent actor. With his face, his eyes. He knows how to use them and how to use his body; he has an innate sense of how much to give and how much to hold back. I look at him, and I know he's a true actor. The camera knows it. And most important, the audience knows it."**

(Go back to page 15.)

Kate Capshaw

Actress Kate Capshaw is best known for her role in the 1984 movie *Indiana Jones and the Temple of Doom*. The film was one of three action movies featuring Harrison Ford as Indiana Jones, and she beat out more than 100 actresses to get the part.

It was on the set of the movie that she met Steven Spielberg, who was directing the film. She knew right away that there was something between her and the director, who was famous for making movies such as *E.T.: The Extra-Terrestrial* and *Close Encounters of the Third Kind*. She and Spielberg married in 1991 and have five children. She also has a daughter from her marriage to Robert Capshaw, which ended in 1980, and is a step-mother to Spielberg's son.

Capshaw was a teacher before she followed her interest in acting. She had a role on the television soap opera *The Edge of Night* in 1981. She also appeared in a number of films and television movies in the 1980s.

After a 19-year absence from the big screen, Indiana Jones returned to the public eye in the 2008 movie *Indiana Jones and the Kingdom of the Crystal Skull*. Spielberg again directed the movie, and Capshaw appeared with him at publicity events for the film.

(Go back to page 17.)

Woody Allen

Tobey Maguire was excited by the chance to work with director Woody Allen on the movie *Deconstructing Harry*. Allen, who has written and directed more than 40 films, is one of the best-known names in American film-making. He is known for putting his own type of thoughtful comedy into his movies.

Allen's real name is Allen Stewart Konigsberg, and he was born in New York in 1935. He began his career in the entertainment industry by writing jokes for television shows. He also worked as a comedian in nightclubs. Allen developed a down-on-his-luck comedy style that carried over into his movies. He did his first movie writing for the 1964 film *What's New, Pussycat?* and also had a small acting role in the film.

Looking for more control over the projects in which he was involved, he wrote his next movie, *What's Up, Tiger Lily?* The movie had been filmed in Japan, but he edited it and added new dialogue.

Allen continued to deliver creative films. In the 1970s his movies included *Play It Again, Sam* and *Manhattan*. *Annie Hall*, released in 1977, won two Academy Awards. Allen also won an Oscar for the 1986 movie *Hannah and Her Sisters*.

(Go back to page 18.)

Ang Lee

Ang Lee, the director of *The Ice Storm*, is known for directing many different types of dramatic films with a sensitive touch. Lee was born on October 23, 1954. He was raised in Taiwan and enrolled in the Taiwan Academy of Art after he failed to get into the national university.

Lee came to the United States in 1981 to study acting. He did not speak English well enough to be an actor, so he turned to directing. He studied at the New York Film School, along with noted director Spike Lee.

He first achieved success in Taiwan with a movie called *Pushing Hands*. He followed it with two more films with Asian themes and then switched gears. He directed Emma Thompson and Kate Winslet in *Sense and Sensibility*. The movie was based on a novel written in 1811 by British writer Jane Austen.

Chinese-born director Ang Lee worked with Tobey Maguire on two films, The Ice Storm *(1997) and* Ride with the Devil *(1999). During his career, Lee has won numerous awards, including Academy Awards for his 2000 film* Crouching Tiger, Hidden Dragon *(Best Foreign Language Film) and 2005's* Brokeback Mountain *(Best Director).*

Lee followed that film with *The Ice Storm*, which is set in America in the 1970s. He directed the Civil War movie *Ride with the Devil* in 1999 and *Crouching Tiger, Hidden Dragon* in 2000.

The director made a superhero film in 2003, *The Hulk*, and a sensitive western, *Brokeback Mountain*, in 2005.

(Go back to page 21.)

Kirsten Dunst

Capturing the role of Mary Jane was a big boost for Kirsten Dunst, but she had a busy career before she was chosen to appear in the *Spider-Man* movies. Dunst, who was born in 1982 in New Jersey, began her acting career as a toddler. She appeared in commercials and signed with the Ford Modeling agency. She got her first movie role in 1989 in Woody Allen's movie *New York Stories*.

Dunst got her big break at age 12 when she beat out 5,000 other young actresses for the role of Claudia in *Interview with a Vampire*. She appeared opposite Brad Pitt and Tom Cruise in the 1994 movie. The movies *Little Women* in 1994 and *Jumanji* in 1995 continued her string of roles in major films.

Dunst kept a very hectic schedule and had to leave her private school and be tutored onset because of her large workload. In 2000 she appeared in *The Crow: Salvation* and *All Forgotten*. She also played an ambitious cheerleader in the movie *Bring It On*.

Kirsten badly wanted the role of Mary Jane. Once she learned Maguire had been cast as Spider-Man, she was eager to act opposite him:

Actress Kirsten Dunst, from a promotional poster for Spider-Man 3. *According to an interview, Dunst wanted Mary Jane to be more than just Spider-Man's girlfriend. She wanted "to make Mary Jane a hero for girls. The boys are going to have Spider-Man and we want Mary Jane to be someone the audience can look up to and believe in."*

❝I had wanted to work with Tobey for the longest time. I always found something very appealing about him. I just had a feeling we'd be really good onscreen together.❞

(Go back to page 29.) ◀◀

Gary Ross

Director Gary Ross started his career as a screenwriter, but he knew early in his career that he wanted to direct. He carefully watched what was going on when he was on the set and learned from what he saw.

Ross first had success writing the script for the movie *Big*, a 1988 comedy that starred Tom Hanks as boy in a man's body. He received an Academy Award nomination for the screenplay as well as a Saturn Award. He also received praise for writing the 1993 movie *Dave*.

His first job as a director came in the 1998 movie *Pleasantville*, which starred Tobey Maguire and Reese Witherspoon. The movie included dazzling special effects as color comes to a black-and-white world.

Ross's next project was to bring the book *Seabiscuit* to the screen. He wrote the screenplay and again asked Maguire to be part of the film. The 2003 movie about a horse, his rider, and owner touched the hearts of audiences. Ross again received an Academy Award nomination for the screenplay for *Seabiscuit*.

In addition to writing and directing his own films, Ross also worked with other writers on movie scripts. He again worked with Maguire on the movie *Tokyo Suckerpunch*.

(Go back to page 32.)

Director Gary Ross at the Seabiscuit *world premiere in 2003. Ross has worked with Tobey Maguire on two major films,* Pleasantville *(1998) and* Seabiscuit *(2003). In both cases, Ross wrote and produced the movies as well as directing them. His other credits include writing the screenplays for the hit films* Big *(1988) and* Dave *(1993).*

Yoga

Yoga is a system of exercises that involves the body and mind. It increases strength and flexibility and relaxes the mind. The practice of yoga began in India thousands of years ago. It was developed as people looked to improve their health and live longer.

Yoga is built on exercise, breathing, and meditation. Exercise makes the body healthy, and controlling breathing can improve the function of the body and mind. Meditation quiets the mind and frees it from stress.

There are many different types of yoga, involving exercises and breathing techniques. Yoga typically involves moving your body into a number of poses. These poses can include the downward dog. This involves placing your hands on the floor and moving them forward. The feet are hip-width apart, and the knees are slightly bent. In this pose, the body looks like it is in an upside-down V shape.

Another pose is the lotus pose. A person is seated to do this pose. The left foot is placed on top of the right thigh, and the right foot is on top of the left thigh. The arms rest on the knees, with palms facing up. The thumb and first finger are touching.

(Go back to page 37.)

Actors/Producers

After the enormous success of the movie *Spider-Man*, Tobey Maguire began producing movies as well as acting in them. He is not the only superstar to go this route. Other actors also have turned to producing in order to be part of the movies they want to make. As actor and producer George Clooney notes,

"It's important to make those films we think are interesting, and we're at a place in our careers and our lives where we can do that."

While actors perform a role onscreen, the producer works behind the scenes. He or she makes business decisions about the movie, including who gets hired and which script is used. The producer also sets pay rates.

Clooney has produced a number of movies, including the 2008 movie *Leatherheads*. He was also the executive producer of the 2007 picture *Michael Clayton* and *Syriana*, released in 2005. Clooney also starred in all of these films.

Movie stars often become producers when they are passionate about a movie. Mexican-American actress Salma Hayek wanted to see a movie made about Mexican artist Frida Kahlo. She worked tirelessly for seven years to bring it to the screen, and she became a producer on the movie that was released in 2002. According to Hayek,

"What is important is to believe in something so strongly that you're never discouraged."

Hayek also starred in *Frida*, but actors do not always star in the films they produce. Brad Pitt did not act in the 2006 movie *The Departed*, but he was one of its producers. That year Clint Eastwood produced the Oscar-nominated movie *Letters from Iwo Jima* but did not act in the film. Eastwood has, however, both starred in and produced the Oscar-winning films *Million Dollar Baby* and *Unforgiven*.

Other actors and actresses who have produced and starred in films include Jennifer Lopez in *Bordertown* and *El Cantante*, Julia Roberts in *Stepmom*, and Leonardo DiCaprio in *The Aviator*.

As producer of *The Aviator*, DiCaprio approached Martin Scorsese about directing the movie and also devoted a great deal of time to researching Howard Hughes, the subject of the movie. It was a process he enjoyed:

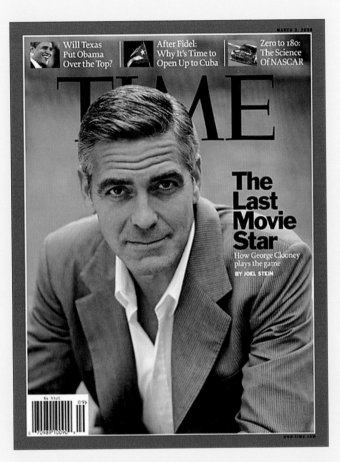

Actor/producer George Clooney is pictured on the cover of this 2008 issue of Time *magazine. Clooney—who worked with Tobey Maguire on* The Good German *(2006)—is one of a growing number of Hollywood stars who have taken a greater role in the way their films are made. Tobey has established a company, Maguire Entertainment, to produce future films.*

"The great thing about movies is you get to immerse yourself in subjects you don't know or are slightly scared of."

(Go back to page 45.) ◀◀

1975 Tobias Maguire is born on June 27, 1975, in Santa Monica, California.

1989 Tobey gets his first acting job in the television special *Rodney Dangerfield: Opening Night at Rodney's Place*.

1990 A number of small roles in television shows come Tobey's way.

1992 Tobey is chosen for the lead in the television series *Great Scott!* but the series is canceled after only a few weeks.

1995 Feeling pressured to succeed and drained by his lifestyle, Maguire asks to be let out of his contract for the movie *Empire Records*.

1996 A new attitude helps Maguire gain acclaim for his work in the short film *The Duke of Groove*.

1997 *The Ice Storm* becomes a breakout role for the actor.

Maguire also gets to work with director Woody Allen on *Deconstructing Harry*.

1998 Maguire has a lead role in *Pleasantville*.

1999 Maguire earns praise for his lead role in *The Cider House Rules*.

2002 *Spider-Man* takes Maguire's career to new heights.

2003 Maguire both acts in and is a producer of the movie *Seabiscuit*.

2004 *Spider-Man 2* is released to great reviews.

2006 Maguire's daughter, Ruby, is born.

2007 Maguire is praised for his work in *Spider-Man 3*.

He marries Jennifer Meyer.

2008 He produces and stars in the movie *Tokyo Suckerpunch*.

1993 Young Artist Award, Best Young Actor in a New Television Series for *Great Scott!* (nominated)

1999 Saturn Award for Best Performance by a Younger Actor/Actress for *Pleasantville*

2000 Toronto Film Critics Association Award, Best Supporting Performance, Male, for *Wonder Boys*
Screen Actors Guild Award, Outstanding Performance by a Cast in a Theatrical Motion Picture for *The Cider House Rules* (nominated)
Teen Choice Awards, Film—Choice Actor for *The Cider House Rules* (nominated) and Film—Choice Liar for *Wonder Boys* (nominated)

2001 Phoenix Film Critics Society Award, Best Actor in a Supporting Role for *Wonder Boys* (nominated)

2002 Teen Choice Awards, Film—Choice Actor, Drama/Action Adventure, Film—Choice Liplock, and Film—Choice Chemistry (nominated), all for *Spider-Man*

2003 MTV Movie Awards, Best Kiss and Best Male Performance (nominated) for *Spider-Man*
Saturn Award, Best Actor for *Spider-Man* (nominated)
Kids' Choice Award, Favorite Male Butt Kicker for *Spider-Man* (nominated)

2004 Screen Actors Guild Award, Outstanding Performance by a Cast in a Motion Picture for *Seabiscuit* (nominated)

2005 Saturn Award for Best Actor for *Spider-Man 2*
Empire Award, Best Actor for *Spider-Man 2* (nominated)
Kids' Choice Award, Favorite Movie Actor (nominated)
People's Choice Award, Favorite Male Action Movie Star for *Spider-Man 2* (nominated)
People's Choice Award, Favorite On-Screen Chemistry for *Spider-Man 2* (nominated)

2007 National Movie Award, Best Performance by a Male for *Spider-Man 3* (nominated)
Teen Choice Awards, Choice Movie Actor: Action Adventure (nominated), Choice Movie: Dance (nominated), Choice Movie: Liplock (nominated), and Choice Movie: Rumble (nominated), all for *Spider-Man 3*

2008 People's Choice Award, Favorite On-Screen Match-Up for *Spider-Man 3* (nominated)

Filmography

1993   *This Boy's Life*

1994   *Healer*
         Revenge of the Red Baron

1996   *Joyride*
         The Duke of Groove

1997   *The Ice Storm*
         Deconstructing Harry

1998   *Fear and Loathing in Las Vegas*
         Pleasantville

1999   *The Cider House Rules*
         Ride with the Devil

2000   *Wonder Boys*

2001   *Don's Plum*
         Cats and Dogs

2002   *Spider-Man*

2003   *Seabiscuit*

2004   *Spider-Man 2*

2006   *The Good German*

2007   *Spider-Man 3*

2008   *Tropic Thunder*
         Brothers
         Tokyo Suckerpunch

Books

Abraham, Philip. *Tobey Maguire*. New York: Children's, 2003.

Wukovits, John. *Tobey Maguire*. Detroit: Lucent, 2006.

Periodicals

Churchill, Bonnie. "It's a Wonder-ful Life for Young Star." *Christian Science Monitor*
    (February 18, 2000): p. 19.

Newsweek. "Tobey Maguire." (May 7, 2007): p. 70.

USA Today. "A Final Spin for Spider-Man?" (July 21, 2006): p. 12D.

Yahlin Chang. "He's Only Too Happy to Be Miserable." *Newsweek* (February 24, 2007): p. 67.

Web Sites

http://spiderman.sonypictures.com

The official Web site of the *Spider-Man* movies.

http://www.imdb.com

The Internet Movie Database contains listings of stars' movies.

http://www.people.com

The Web site for *People* magazine has the latest information on the activities of
famous people.

http://www.themovieinsider.com

The Movie Insider provides information on the latest films and movies in production.

Publisher's note:

The Web sites mentioned in this book were active at the time of publication. The publisher is not responsible
for Web sites that have changed their addresses or discontinued operation since the date of publication.
The publisher will review and update the Web site addresses each time the book is reprinted.

audition—to try out for a role in a television show or movie.

blockbuster—a very successful film.

budget—the amount of money available for a movie.

critic—a person who reviews a movie and offers an opinion.

director—a person who oversees the making of a show and offers advice on how a scene should be played.

episode—one show in a series.

nominated—proposed as a candidate for an award.

producer—a person who oversees or provides money for a television show, movie, or play.

role—a part in a show played by an actress or actor.

sequel—a movie, television show, or book that continues a story from a previous work and uses the same characters.

sitcom—a situation comedy. A television comedy series that features the same, or almost the same, cast of characters and setting in each episode.

special effects—sights and sounds added to a movie.

typecast—to often cast an actress or actor in similar roles.

villains—evil characters.

page 6 "It seems fans everywhere . . ." "His World Wide Web," *Maclean's* (May 21, 2007): p. 12.

page 6 "pretty stressed out . . ." Sean Smith and Devin Gordon, "Tobey Maguire: *Spider-Man 2.*" *Newsweek* (May 10, 2004): p. 53.

page 9 "We really show the awesome . . ." Mike Snider, "*Spider-Man 3* Uses Sand to Great Effect." *USA Today* (May 14, 2007): p. 8D.

page 9 "There is kind of a Goth . . . " "Tobey Maguire," *Newsweek* (May 7, 2007): p. 70.

page 9 "Maguire somehow still makes us . . ." Kevin Lally, "*Spider-Man 3.*" *Film Journal International* (June 2007): p. 36.

page 11 "By the time . . ." Ingrid Sischy, "Maguire Fire." *Interview* (October 1998): p. 142.

page 11 "Watching Leo was great . . ." Sischy, "Maguire Fire," p. 142.

page 12 "It was so exciting . . ." Bonnie Churchill, "It's a Wonder-ful Life for Young Star." *Christian Science Monitor* (February 18, 2000): p. 19.

page 12 "I was so excited . . ." "Tobey Maguire," *Newsweek*, p. 70.

page 15 "I had to make a . . ." John Brodie, "The Immaculate Ascension of Tobey Maguire." *GQ* (March 2003): p. 286.

page 16 "It all came from . . ." Dave Karger, "Tobey or Not Tobey." *Entertainment Weekly* (March 3, 2000): p. 38.

page 18 "I happen to be blessed   . . ." Yahlin Chang, "He's Only Too Happy to Be Miserable." *Newsweek* (February 24, 2007): p. 67.

page 19 "Maguire, with his sweet . . ." Lisa Schwarzbaum, "In Living Color." *Entertainment Weekly* (October 30, 1998): p. 77.

page 21 "For me personally . . ." Deanna Kizis, "Cosmo Q&A." *Cosmopolitan* (May 1999): p. 214.

page 21 "Maguire acquires a new, leaner . . ." Lisa Schwarzbaum, "Wild Orchard." *Entertainment Weekly* (December 17, 1999): p. 58.

page 22 "captivating and creepy . . ." Peter Travers, "Movies." *Rolling Stone* (March 16, 2000): p. 81.

page 22 "This young actor . . ." Owen Gleiberman, "Guy, Interrupted." *Entertainment Weekly* (February 25, 2000): p. 52.

page 22 "One of the things . . ." Lev Grossman, "Tobey Grows Up." *Time South Pacific* (July 28, 2003): p. 62.

page 23 "I'm really with the pros . . ." Churchill, "It's a Wonder-ful Life for Young Star," p. 19.

page 25 "I can be pretty subtle . . ." Dave Karger, "Tobey or Not Tobey." *Entertainment Weekly* (March 3, 2000): p. 38.

page 25 "I have faith that nothing . . ." Churchill, "It's a Wonder-ful Life for Young Star," p. 19.

page 27 "Spider-Man for me . . ." Ferguson, "The Man Behind the Mask," p. 24.

page 28 "He's got magnetism . . ." *People*, "Tobey Maguire." (June 24, 2002): p. 73.

page 28 "I look forward to . . ." Ferguson, "The Man Behind the Mask," p. 24.

page 29 "As a child . . ." Tom Russo, "Swing Time: What a Costume Drama! All the Superheroics Behind Spider-Man's Leap to the Big Screen." *Entertainment Weekly* (April 26, 2002): p. 38.

page 31 "I wait. I don't want . . . " Grossman, "Tobey Grows Up," p. 62.

page 31 "It's very much . . . " Steven Kotler, "A Hero's Ride." *Variety* (April 7, 2003): p. 8.

page 32 "It's not just about winning . . . " Sheryl Berk, "Tobey Maguire Racing to the Top." *Biography* (August 2003): p. 36.

page 35 "When he doubts himself . . . " Lisa Schwarzbaum, "Spin City." *Entertainment Weekly* (July 9, 2004): p. 59.

page 38 "Let's just say . . . " William Keck, "Jennifer Meyer Sparkles." *USA Today* (July 12, 2006): p. 3D.

page 39 "Steven Soderbergh tries . . . " Todd McCarthy, "*The Good German*." *Variety* (December 4, 2006): p. 55.

page 40 "I do the stuff that . . . " Scott Huver, "The Last Web Crawl?" *Tribute* (April 2007): p. 18.

page 40 "It is important . . . " Huver, "The Last Web Crawl?" p. 18.

page 43 "Somehow this ambitious . . . " David Ansen, "Spidey the Swinger." *Newsweek* (May 7, 2007): p. 60.

page 43 "It's hard to imagine . . . " *USA Today*, "A Final Spin for Spider-Man?" (July 21, 2006): p. 12D.

page 47 "I finally told myself . . ." Sam Raimi, "What a Web He Weaves." *Entertainment Weekly* (May 3, 2002): p. 92.

page 49 "He Holds the screen . . ." Martin Scorsese, "Leonardo DiCaprio." *Time* (May 14, 2007): p. 150.

page 52 "to make Mary Jane . . ." David Keeps, "Kirsten Dunst Busts Out." *Rolling Stone* (May 23, 2002): p. 62.

page 52 "I had wanted to work . . . " David Keeps, "Kirsten Dunst Busts Out." *Rolling Stone.* (May 23, 2002): p. 62.

page 54 "It's important to make . . . " Sharon Knolle, "Multitasking Marvels," *Daily Variety* (November 28, 2005): p. A16.

page 55 "What is important . . . " Bonnie Laufer-Krebs, "Salma Hayek." *Tribute* (November 2002): p. 33.

page 55 "The great thing . . . " Stephen Galloway, "Leonardo DiCaprio." *Hollywood Reporter* (January 4, 2005): p. 35.

Numbers in ***bold italics*** refer to captions.

Terri Dougherty has written more than 60 books for children. She lives in Appleton, Wisconsin, with her husband, Denis, and their three children. They are all fans of the *Spider-Man* movies and enjoy watching them together.

PICTURE CREDITS

page

1: Columbia Pictures/NMI

4: Columbia Pictures/NMI

7: Columbia Pictures/NMI

8: Columbia Pictures/NMI

10: ASP/PRMS

13: MCA Special Products/PRMS

14: Warner Bros./NMI

16: ASP/PRMS

19: Fox Searchlight Pictures/WENN

20: New Line Cinema/NMI

23: Paramount Pictures/NMI

24: FilmMagic

26: Columbia Pictures/NMI

29: Columbia Pictures/FilmMagic

30: Columbia Pictures/FilmMagic

32: Universal Studios/NMI

34: Fashion Wire Daily

35: Columbia Pictures/NMI

36: Jemal Countess/WireImage

39: Warner Bros./NMI

41: Premiere/NMI

42: Columbia Pictures/NMI

44: PopSugar/CIC Photos

47: Columbia Pictures/NMI

49: 20th Century Fox/NMI

51: Focus Features/PRMS

52: Columbia Pictures/NMI

53: Kevin Winter/Getty Images

55: Time/NMI

Front cover: Columbia Pictures/NMI